Someone I Know Is Dying

Practical Advice from an

End-of-Life Companion

Someone I Know
Is Dying

Practical Advice
from an End-of-Life
Companion

Priscilla Ronan

Published in Phoenix, Arizona by Parola Publishing.

ISBN 978-0-9909238-0-0

Printed in the United States of America

First Edition 10 9 8 7 6 5 4 3 2 1

To my husband, Emmet,

whose love and support

paved the way for this book.

Table of Contents

INTRODUCTION:

Witnessing the Dying Process

It is an honor to be part of someone's dying process.

"Are you afraid?" Violet's roommate asks me as she slowly wheels herself across the small bedroom in the assisted living facility. Her voice cuts into the silence in the sparsely furnished room.

The question interrupts the sound of Violet's labored breathing as I sit holding her carefully manicured hand. Her hands are still warm, and one finger glistens with a beautiful amethyst ring.

I answer automatically, "No, I'm not afraid."

As a hospice volunteer, I am sitting with Violet as she dies to keep her from being alone. She might die during the time I'm with her or linger for a few days.

Violet's roommate wheels herself out of the room, and I begin to think about being afraid. What does her roommate mean? Am I afraid of being with Violet when she dies? Am I afraid of death?

There are other questions, of course. How can you feel comfortable being with someone who is dying? What are the right things to say and to do? What is your role in the dying process for this person? How can you take care of yourself while being a caregiver to someone near the end of life?

These are just a few of the questions I'll answer in this book.

What we know for certain is that death touches everyone. And it is much more than the dictionary definition—"the time when something ends"—or a medical event. Dying involves both the person leaving and the loved ones left behind. Sharing in a person's final hours can be a peaceful or even a joy-filled event.

. . .

I'm an ordinary person—a wife and mother of four sons, a mother-in-law, and a grandmother. I don't have a medical background. In fact, I'm a teacher by education, a business owner, a corporate trainer, a writer, and a public speaker.

And for over twenty-five years, I have been with numerous people (and their families) at the end of their lives—for ten years as a hospice volunteer and before that, twenty years in non-hospice-related care for the dying. Through my volunteer work with a hospice I have received training regarding end of life and dying, and for more than seven years I have spoken to various groups in the Greater Phoenix area dispelling the myths surrounding hospice care and discussing the process of dying. Throughout my observation and experience in a variety of circumstances, I kept a journal—not only about what was happening while someone was dying or at the death, but also about the things that helped me, the dying person, and anyone else I interacted with at the time.

You may find yourself a part of someone's dying experience (a parent, a spouse, a sibling, or a friend). It may be part of your job to be with someone who is nearing death, as a hospice or health care worker, doctor, nurse, or volunteer. There is an art to being present and reflecting life for someone. This may be someone who is close to you or who might even be a stranger, but nonetheless becomes part of your life story as you witness his or her dying process.

Just as baby books tell you the stages of a child's development, you may have been told the steps toward death: denial, rage and anger, bargaining, depression, and acceptance. My experience is that sometimes these steps occur and sometimes they do not—anything is possible. Death is similar to the labor of giving birth; there are many variations. Some people follow a predictable path, but death is always a unique experience.

We all will face death at some point in our lives—our own, of course, but more than likely someone we love will precede us. And the living—the end-of-life companions—find themselves without a guide. I have read a variety of books about death and dying and could not find a simple, easy-to-read book that addressed the concerns of a person watching a loved one nearing the end of life.

Most of us are unprepared for this role. This book attempts to provide some practical solutions. Some ideas may work for you, and some may not. Don't be afraid to try something new that may be helpful during your time spent with someone who is busy dying. Remember that this time will be difficult and challenging, but it can also be a time of learning about ourselves and how we prepare for facing death as part of life.

How This Book Is Organized

Someone I Know Is Dying:
Practical Advice from an End-of-Life Companion
is divided into three parts.

PART ONE is about **choosing the role you take** when interacting with someone who is dying. You may be a reluctant participant in someone's dying process or a passionate advocate or caregiver for a close relative or friend. It may even be part of your job to interact with someone who is near death. This book provides questions to ask yourself and practical solutions—whether you step in unexpectedly, show up at the right time, or find yourself to be the decision maker. Each story helps you to navigate your way through the ups and downs associated with being in a particular role.

PART TWO helps you **determine what to do and say** in various situations surrounding the dying process. From understanding the dying process to discovering what matters most in life and death, from listening with your whole body to sitting in silence, from learning how to have a beginner's mind and an awareness of what your body is telling you, each chapter provides you with tools and helps you find the words and right actions in many types of difficult situations.

PART THREE is about learning **how to care for yourself** during an often very difficult and demanding time. The focus of this section is about you, the one who is interacting with the dying person. Think about your limits and develop a plan that keeps you healthy and sane. Set clear boundaries and be kind to yourself. Each chapter allows you to learn and practice techniques to help yourself and the person who is dying.

PART ONE:

Choosing Your Role

Choosing Your Role

Understand the gift of freedom.

*You are free to choose
what to do, where to go, and your attitude—
no matter what is happening.*

"You are not allowed to be sick and die before me!" Tom's elderly mom yells at him over the phone. Tom is a middle-aged married man told by his doctors that he has less than one week to live.

When I meet Tom, he tells me he is working toward healing and health. His goals are simple: to provide for his wife, to be able to take care of himself, and to enjoy the simple pleasures of life.

He keeps imploring me to tell people that if they don't learn to "let go" and really figure out how to live their lives simply and fully, they're going to end up like him: reluctantly dying at a young age.

Tom is a corporate executive who was married previously. There are some difficulties in how his sons from that first marriage are dealing with his illness. Obviously Tom's mother is having a very difficult time. She calls him and yells at him for being so sick. She cannot fathom the thought that her son will die before she does.

Many families have these types of stories.

What Is My Role?

What is my role in Tom's dying process? My role appears to be as an observer of the action and as a helper for his family to let him go. I encourage each person who visits Tom to be present to him, listen to him, and simply love him. I ask his family and friends to treat him with respect—and follow his lead.

Tom is a person used to being in charge at work and at home. He doesn't want his wife taking care of his bodily needs. Other support people from the health care service and hospice can shave and bathe him, allowing him some dignity during his last days.

His wife feels such relief knowing that it is okay to just sit with him, hold his hand, and to quietly be with Tom in his final days.

Tom dies peacefully, with his wife supporting him in love. The day after his death, a bouquet of flowers from Tom to his wife arrives. He dies as he lived, taking care of and thinking about his wife.

In this situation, I had a clear role. However, that role may not be so simple and clear-cut for the person helping the family or for the family experiencing an untimely death.

We All Have a Part to Play—Large or Small

Your role will reveal itself depending on your relationship with the dying person. How you *respond* to that role is your choice. In Tom's circumstance, I truly was an observer, since I did not know much about Tom or his life. A friend of mine felt concerned that Tom's wife was not allowing anyone to help her during Tom's final days. Whenever I entered Tom's home, I asked him if he wanted me to sit and talk with him. Since he agreed, I could listen to what Tom wanted in his final days. My role began with an agreement between Tom and myself. I asked him at the end of our first visit if he would like me to visit him again. Since he answered yes, I called each time before I visited to make sure that Tom was agreeable to a short visit from me.

If you are part of the family and pulled into all the family drama and past roles each of you played during your time together, it is still your choice to take the role that is most beneficial to you and to your loved one. I observed Tom, his wife and one of his grown sons during my early visits to his home. His son rented funny television shows and movies that the family enjoyed when the son was growing up. After asking me if I thought it was all right, the son crawled into the hospital bed in the living room so that father and son could watch and laugh at the programs. This act of companionship and laughter made both father and son more comfortable with Tom's dying process.

You may feel pressure from others regarding the role you play. Tom's other sons did not visit him; they arrived after he died. Remember, your role is not to judge others' behavior in the dying person's process.

What Is Most Helpful?
Do That.

If you are comfortable sitting and listening to the dying person, then do so. If you're uncomfortable in that role, then find something else to do to be of service to the family. I was available to visit Tom each day during his final week of life. Of course, I didn't know that he had only one week to live. I would ask his wife if she would like me to visit Tom sometime during each day. If the answer was no, I did not intrude into their lives. I appreciated his wife's honesty with me.

When I arrived at Tom's home, I asked his wife what would be most helpful for me to do during my visit. Most of the time, she wanted me to sit with Tom. At other times, she wanted to sit with Tom after I listened to her worries about him. I did not need to be the nurse, doctor, or social worker— just a friend who reinforced what Tom's wife already knew she wanted and needed.

Sometimes, Tom enjoyed talking to me, telling me about his life, and allowing me to massage his legs. When he could no longer talk, I would listen to other family members and friends of the family.

It's often as simple as that. Think about what you feel comfortable doing and what you don't want to do. It's okay to say no. Often this takes practice if you aren't accustomed to saying no to others. If you find you can't help or don't know how to help, find out about resources available in your community. A phone call to a hospice agency or community resource center can give you helpful ideas and information.

Again, choose your attitude. In his book *Man's Search for Meaning*, Viktor Frankl, a famous psychiatrist who survived a World War II concentration camp, talks about the one human freedom that cannot be taken away from a person: his or her attitude in any given circumstance. In this case, we remember that in our encounter with the dying person, we have a choice in the attitude we take toward that role.

• • •

The chapters in
PART ONE: Choosing Your Role
will look at some of the circumstances and roles
you might find yourself in.

PART ONE

CHAPTER 1:

When to Step In

What matters most in life
is when we are there for someone else
with kind words and loving actions.

It's early Monday morning and I wake up with a dream about Sue, a woman I met a few months before. I know she is dying of lung cancer. In the dream, I see and hear her calling me to be with her. I remember when I wake up that Sue is now quite sick and is at her home near death.

I recall meeting Sue when she was in remission for her cancer. She animatedly talked to me about how she was savoring each day: the simple blessings in her life, making each moment count, and taking the time to "smell the roses."

Early in her cancer diagnosis, Sue made plans for her funeral, chose her gravesite, and said good-bye to her family and friends with a big party. The party celebrated her time with her family and friends. She knew that she would not remain in "good health" forever.

This early morning when I visit her, she is curled up on her side with labored breathing, nearing her death. I play soft music, hold her hand, and sit quietly with her. I follow her breathing and at times breathe along with her. I gaze into her eyes and speak silently from my heart to hers. At times, I rub her arms and face with my hands. There is a feeling of joy and love in the room and in the house. The world seems to stop and revolve around this beautiful woman in the bed.

These are truly the final hours of her life. Her husband allows me to sit quietly with her as he finishes washing and folding clothes. I continue breathing with her and notice that when Sue's husband comes into the room she appears to be in pain. When I am leaving to return to my home, I advise him to talk to Sue out loud or silently, breathe with her, and let her know that it's okay to leave. She dies only a few hours after I return home.

Questions to Ask Yourself

How do I know when to step in?

This story begins with me waking up and dreaming about Sue. We often discard our premonitions and dreams when we are thinking of loved ones or friends who are terminally ill. For some reason, we don't think about following our gut-level feelings or intuition. Intuition is simply using a purposeful impulse to carry out an action.

When Sue was dying, I called her husband to ask about visiting her. He told me she was in a coma and I could visit her if I wished. I followed my intuition to visit, and it was the right thing to do.

How are the people around me responding to my helpfulness?

Even though you may wish to be present to offer comfort and support as someone approaches the end of their life, you must respect the dying person's wishes. As one of my close friends lay dying in a nearby hospital, I was able to speak on the phone with her daughter. As we hung up, I felt that I should go be with the family and visit my friend, perhaps for the last time. When I arrived at the hospital, my dying friend's brother told me that she only wanted immediate family in her room. I sat quietly in the waiting room and respected my friend's last wishes.

The dying person often desires to maintain some type of control as his or her world diminishes. I had to remind myself that this was not a time for me to decide what needed to be done or what I wished I could do. By being there, I was not helping my friend, but rather my friend's daughter when her mother finally died.

What to Remember

Use your intuition, gut feeling,
or instincts to guide you in
knowing when to step in.

You are there to be of service
and help to the dying person and
his or her family members.

• • •

Sometimes it's difficult to respect the
wishes of the dying person and his or her family.
It's a time to truly understand that
this process is not about you.

CHAPTER 2:

Showing Up at the Right Time

Whatever happens,
sink into the place that feels right
and know you have done your best.
Just show up and
notice what life presents.

Sally, Sam's wife, attends a public seminar I teach called *Life Design: Creating the Adventure of Your Life*. During one of the breaks, Sally tells me about her husband, who is having some heart problems. I tell her that if she ever needs me, to please call. This isn't a time in my life when I am thinking that I "work" with people who are dying. I am a trainer helping people transition in their careers.

A few weeks later, Sally calls me one evening from a local hospital and says that Sam is not expected to live through the night. I leave my husband with our four young sons and go to the hospital. During the drive to the hospital, I focus myself and realize that all I need to do is to follow Sally's lead and be there for her. She is alone and quite distraught when I meet her outside the intensive care area. We sit in the waiting room, as only immediate family members are allowed in Sam's hospital room.

I ask her: "What if this is truly the last night for Sam? What would you want to have happen?"

She immediately answers: "I want him to know how much I love him. I want to hold his hand and be with him, no matter what happens."

I reinforce what Sally already wants to do. She spends the night in Sam's intensive care hospital room doing exactly what she tells me she wants to do. Miraculously, Sam survives the night and eventually progresses and is released from the hospital. At times, impending death for a person can unexpectedly become a temporary reprieve, and life continues.

Questions to Ask Yourself

How do I know when I am showing up at the right time?

The offer to support someone when his or her loved one is sick needs to be a genuine offer of help. You do not need any particular training in order to help another person. Show up and be a good listener. Often the person just needs someone to listen and help sort out the next steps.

A hospital can be an overwhelming place for the person who is asked to make decisions regarding a near-death patient. And the dying process can seem mysterious. Even trained hospice personnel do not always know the time for someone's death.

What if a miracle occurs and the dying person gets better?

In this story, a miracle does occur, and Sam recovers. We often hear these types of stories. If you miraculously have the chance to spend more time with a dying loved one, savor each and every moment.

What if the person is truly near death and I'm not sure what to do?

Being there as an observer of the process can be exactly what is needed at the moment. Not interfering, but supporting family members can be very comforting to them. If you are the only one with the dying person, your presence (and touch, if appropriate) can make the end of life a time of peacefulness and joy instead of fear and loneliness. Read Chapter 7 in this book for more ideas about what to do.

How can I prepare myself when I "show up" or visit a dying person?

If you are anxious about visiting, talk with someone who knows about the person's condition. Maybe you don't want to visit alone. For example, my sister's best friend was very ill, and my sister asked if I would go with her to visit her friend.

Call and ask if it's a good time to visit. Ask again when you arrive and be prepared to wait or come back another time.

At this point in the dying person's life, the focus is on his or her needs and wishes. Often visits are short, since the person most likely tires easily and might even sleep throughout your time together.

What should I talk about?

Take cues from the person. Perhaps he or she wants to just sit quietly, or listen to music or watch television. For conversations, talk about your memories of the person and recollect and remember good times you've shared. Bringing and sharing photos can be a great conversation starter. Read the chapters in Part Two of this book for more ideas on what to say.

What to Remember

Sometimes the caregiver for the dying person
needs to be listened to and encouraged
to follow his or her instincts and wishes
for being with the dying person.

• • •

Many dying people do not want to be alone
or in pain during the end of their lives,
and your presence can make a difference
in managing their fears.

• • •

You can relieve the anxiety of
loved ones with your calm demeanor
and ability to listen.
Remember that you are not giving answers

but instead providing a safe
sounding board for their concerns.

• • •

The focus is on the
dying person's needs and wishes
so be prepared
to change your plans
for visiting or helping.

• • •

Relax and observe what the person wants to do.
Take cues from the dying person for hugging,
holding hands, and other signs of affection.
If the person is unconscious, you might
ask someone who knows the person if
he or she liked to be touched
before he or she became ill.

• • •

Listen, talk if appropriate,
and know that
sitting in silence is okay.

CHAPTER 3:

The Player on the Stage

The power of our
attitude toward life is immense.
We are like players on a stage and how we
perform our part is the very challenge and essence of life.
There is a space between our action and reaction.
Use that space wisely.

The craziness of balancing family, work, and outside activities often feels like I'm spinning too many plates—and that one is sure to fall at any moment.

After a week of more activities than usual, I stop at a favorite yogurt shop on my way to an evening out with some friends. I sit relaxing in the quiet shop, barely noticing the few people eating and talking at other tables. Out of the corner of my eye, I notice a woman, young child, and a man. The man suddenly falls out of his chair, and the woman frantically leans over him. Someone in the shop calls an ambulance. As the EMTs care for the man and get him into the ambulance, I step in to help by taking care of the child.

The distraught woman tells me that they have walked to the yogurt shop from a nearby apartment complex. I offer to drive her to the emergency room and help her call a neighbor who agrees to watch the child.

At the emergency room, the woman, Lisa, is told that her husband, Brad, has suffered a major heart attack and that when he is stabilized she can join him. I calmly sit with her, holding her hand, listening as she tells me the story about Brad and their child, Molly. I learn about Brad's older children from an earlier marriage who are not in contact with him at this time.

My intuition is to tell her that when she sees Brad she is to talk to him even if he is unconscious and unresponsive. She can let Brad know that she and Molly are all right.

The doctors tell Lisa that Brad most likely will not survive this attack. I support Lisa by sitting with her as she calls out-of-state family members with the news.

When Brad is generally stabilized and Lisa is ready to return home, I drop her at her apartment and leave my name and contact information in case she wants to talk again in the future.

A few weeks go by, and I watch the obituaries for Brad's name to appear but never see it. A few months later, I receive a phone call from Brad himself saying that he would like to meet me! Brad survived the heart attack and had time to remedy some family difficulties.

My role in this situation was to act in the moment and then allow other people to step in and play other roles in Lisa and Brad's lives.

Questions to Ask Yourself

How can I be of service to someone in the moment?

There were other people in the yogurt shop who sat back and watched the events. As a mother of four young sons, it was easy for me to step in and comfort the young child. I could also ask if the wife needed some assistance. In this circumstance, this consisted of giving her a ride and helping her call a neighbor.

How do I know what to offer and to do?

Do what you are comfortable offering and doing. There have been other emergencies when I watched others take care of people. Notice what is not being done and then step in and offer your help if appropriate. Know that it's all right to assess the situation and then step away when your services are not needed. It's important to respect any professionals who are dealing with the emergency.

What to Remember

Your role in an emergency
is not always clearly defined.
Step in when your help is accepted.

Stay close by and notice what is
not being offered or done.

• • •

Don't interfere with any professionals
who are dealing with the emergency.

• • •

We play many parts or
roles in our lives.
I like to think about
Shakespeare's play
As You Like It,
where we have our
entrances and exits
like players on a stage.
When it's our turn,
we should gracefully enter—
and then leave when our part is done.

• • •

My favorite Zen saying is:
Step forward with your heart and act.
Don't wait around
for anyone from above
to give you a signal.

CHAPTER 4:

The Advocate

*To support and assure, to intercede
and translate intention:
this is the true gift of friendship
in times of difficulty.*

"This time I am done. No more procedures. I am going to put everything in order and hope that I have a few weeks left."

Linda takes charge of almost everything in her life. She is a tireless worker. As a single divorced mother, she cares for her handicapped daughter and provides a home for her son. In the past year, another son has died from complications of an accident that left him a paraplegic. Linda is truly an advocate for the people in her life.

This time as she enters the hospital, she asks me to be her advocate as she faces a recurrence of colon cancer. Linda makes lists of questions for the doctors regarding her treatment and recovery. She is preparing to take charge and get well soon. As Linda opens doors toward her own recovery, she is making lists for her daughter's care, for her business, and for her son and his young family.

As she recovers in her hospital bed from surgery, a doctor tells her about the recurrence of her cancer and of the possibility of another surgery that might prolong her life for perhaps a few more months. Linda decides that she does not have the strength for more medical interventions.

So this time, I am not a hospice volunteer but a close friend who becomes Linda's advocate in her final days. Most of the decisions are Linda's to make, and I am the person to carry out her final wishes.

She decides during this time in the hospital that she is not going home to die. She asks to go to a "hospice home" for her final days. She has already planned for her family's future through her will and insurance policies. As hospice is called in, she answers questions about plans for cremation, no funeral and her ashes in her "box" (already picked out and paid for), traveling to her native state. She dies peacefully surrounded by her family, including her dogs.

Questions to Ask Yourself

What is my role as an advocate?

An advocate is someone who speaks for and carries out the

dying person's wishes. An advocate may have to ask difficult questions. In this circumstance, my friend wanted me to ask medical personnel certain questions and relay the answers to her. An advocate may discover missed details, such as medications prescribed but not given/taken appropriately.

Being an advocate means making sure that you follow through and understand what is important to the dying person. It's being respectful of hospital personnel but ensuring that procedures are followed correctly.

An advocate sees to it that the dying person is relatively pain free and cared for throughout the dying process.

Your role is not to be demanding. It's to be able to verify that the right medications are given to keep the dying person comfortable. You may want to ask an indirect question if you are dealing with staff. For example: "I'm wondering if (insert dying person's name) is in pain. What do you think?", rather than "This person needs medication right now!"

One time when I was in a dying person's home and the woman's son was not sure if he should give her the medication, I asked him what his thoughts were about the medication. He was worried that his mother would "get hooked." He needed reassurance that the medicine was intended to keep his mother comfortable, as she was very near death at that time.

What about how I feel about the dying person's wishes?

As an advocate, you need to be clear about what the dying person wants. This means dropping your personal thoughts or judgments and advocating for the person's final wishes.

What to Remember

Take your cues from the dying person.
It is not a case of what is right or wrong.
When the person is done
trying procedures and therapies,
respect that choice.

• • •

You can check with hospital personnel
or caretakers regarding pain relief
and ask how often medication can be given.
Often near the end of someone's life,
the orders for medication change
to provide additional comfort.
This might not be conveyed
to the right people attending to the person
you are advocating for.

• • •

It is all right to check with the staff about
medications and times given to the patient.
Ask questions in a caring,
not demanding, tone.

• • •

Be an advocate who influences
rather than demands.

• • •

Educate yourself regarding
end-of-life medicines.

• • •

Pay attention to how the
dying person is responding.
Your role as an advocate
is to make sure that the dying person
is comfortable.

• • •

Make sure that the dying person's
wants and final wishes
are being followed
by everyone.

CHAPTER 5:

The Referee

*Go face to face
with the fragility of life.*

As a hospice volunteer, sitting with someone who is dying tends to be a very quiet peaceful time for me. I arrive at the facility, usually an assisted living residence, with a roll cart. Inside the cart I have my "box of things to do while I sit." Generally I have a good book, a music player with some favorite quiet relaxing music, some snacks and a bottle of water (for me). I am given the name, diagnosis, age of the person who is actively dying, and whether he or she has any relatives. Often the people I visit are alone, having outlived most of their friends, and their immediate family members may live out of town.

I am to make sure the dying person is comfortable, which means that pain medication is given as prescribed by the doctor. At times, I play quiet music, and sometimes I may even read aloud if the person's family has requested certain books. Perhaps a favorite show is on television. The best times for me are when I can sit quietly, holding the person's hand. I speak gently to the person, saying that I am there and will not leave. My volunteer time is a four-hour vigil. Sometimes the person may die when I'm there, whereas at other times, I'm one of a series of volunteers who sit with the person until the death.

This time, when I arrive, the gentleman is very near death. The nurse at the facility tells me that his wife died a few weeks earlier and there is one daughter who is grateful that I can sit with her father, since she needs to work on this day. Next I am told that another daughter is not allowed to visit. In fact, there is a restraining order against her, and I am to make sure she does not see her father or gain any information about him.

I sit down, realizing that I am part of this person's life story and need to let my own misgivings about the family dynamics not influence my sitting and being present for this particular man's dying process.

Questions to Ask Yourself

What is my "referee" role if there are extraordinary circumstances surrounding the death of the person I'm with?

In this circumstance, I'm given information that is uncomfortable for me personally, since I don't even know either daughter. However, the focus should always be on the dying person. Find out what you can do to make the dying person comfortable and not feel the stress of the outside world. My focus is on being present to the dying man and his comfort.

How can I be a referee?

In sports, a referee is an official who enforces the rules. I think of a referee for a dying person as the one who makes sure that the "rules" for the dying person are followed. This means that the dying person is allowed to experience a peaceful, comfortable death.

In business, you often need to get past the "gatekeeper" to speak or visit with the person in charge of the business. Your role as referee is to be this gatekeeper for the dying person.

One dying woman I visited was quite popular in her assisted living complex and people kept stopping by to "see how she was doing." Her daughter noticed how agitated her mother became with each visit, and asked me if it would be okay to put a note on the door stating that it was not a good time to visit. The simple note on the door allowed her mother to die in peace.

What if I am part of the family dynamics?

It's more difficult to be the referee when you are part of the family dynamics. Get someone outside of your family to help. This may be a professional counselor or mediator.

When my mother was ill, my three sisters and I had varying points of view on how to proceed with her care. A professional counselor who dealt primarily with elder care issues helped us sort out our various roles. The counselor became the referee and reference point for us in making decisions. This way we didn't get caught up in our regular family roles and positions.

What to Remember

The referee for the dying person
is often a mediator and protector.
You can oversee and make sure
that the dying person is safe and
surrounded by those people who can
support and love him or her
without causing undue
stress or harm.

• • •

If you are part of the family dynamics,
perhaps an outside person (or professional help)
can serve as a referee or mediator if necessary.

• • •

Understand and be clear about what
the "rules" are for the dying person.

CHAPTER 6:

The Decision Maker

*Adjusting to circumstances, determining what
needs to be done: this is how to move forward in life.*

"I just don't understand why she won't use a feeding tube. I don't want her to die." Karen's daughter is distraught that her mother has decided that she is finished with all methods to prolong her life.

Eighty-year-old Karen is resting peacefully in her bed at an assisted living facility. Her daughter, Lynn, describes her mother as an energetic, feisty woman. She can't understand why her mother has "given up" and is ready to die.

In this case, the dying person made the decision to stop the doctors from inserting a feeding tube. I step outside Karen's room with Lynn and listen to her talk about her mother and the past few years. As Lynn discusses her mother and her life, she calms down and realizes that Karen is still making her own decisions. She may not agree with Karen's end-of-life decisions, but she must honor them, even if it's painful for her to watch.

A thirteen-year-old friend of one of my sons suddenly lapses into a coma and is at a hospital near my home. When I arrive at the hospital to check on her welfare, the parents meet me in the hallway. After hugs and many tears, Terry's parents tell me that the doctors have just given them no hope for her recovery. It is time to let all of the machines keeping her breathing be turned off. Being the decision maker in this case is heartbreaking.

In another circumstance, an elderly friend is ready to die after various treatments have not stopped the progression of his cancer. Barry decides, along with his family, that he does not want any more treatments to prolong his life. As Barry nears death and appears uncomfortable to the family members, a doctor suggests a new treatment. Barry is unconscious and unresponsive at this time, and the family decides to go along with the doctor's new treatment idea. At the last minute, Barry's wife remembers his intentions and decides to honor her husband's request for no more treatments.

Questions to Ask Yourself

Who is the decision maker?

Sometimes it's the dying person who makes final decisions regarding treatment. At other times it's the family, a family member, or a friend. That individual can have the legal right to make decisions or simply be the point person responsible for gathering information to give to the dying person and/or family and friends.

What if my role is the decision maker?

The best solution for the decision maker is to think about what the dying person has requested or stated, either formally or informally. Decision makers both think with their heads and listen to their hearts.

Keep a list of things that need to be done if you are the decision maker. If this is your role, make sure all legal documents that specify the dying person's wishes are signed and completed. These can include medical power of attorney and living will information.

Your list can also include questions to ask professionals, financial considerations, and various practical needs, such as beds, equipment, and food. Identify people who might be helpful and can complete some of these items on the list.

Make a list of ways to begin the conversation regarding items that can (and need to) be done with the dying person. This list can include sorting through photo albums and memorabilia, final wishes about eulogies, services, and those people the person might want to talk to or have visit before his or her final days.

What if I am the decision maker and feel overwhelmed?

If you're feeling overwhelmed and not sure about what the next steps should be, accept your feelings; then consider that this may be the right time to get some outside advice. There are professional services available in most areas. A call to a hospice in your area can direct you to many free or cost-saving services.

What to Remember

Being a decision maker is not always easy.
Following someone's wishes when your heart
is breaking is not a simple task.

• • •

Be clear on what the dying person wants.
It is best to discuss this before the
dying person's final days.

• • •

If legal documents need to be signed,
do that ahead of time and have the documents
available for hospital personnel or
emergency technicians.

• • •

Hospice is a good place to ask for help and services.
Find out what resources are available in your area
to help with decision making.

PART TWO:

Knowing What to
Do and Say

Knowing What to Do and Say

Speak your truth and
then get out of the way.
Accept all that is unfolding,
take appropriate action,
and allow life to deliver the story.

"I just can't seem to do crossword puzzles anymore. I can't think of the words. It's so frustrating when you get old."

My ninety-three-year-old friend, formerly a therapist, sits in a wheelchair in an assisted living facility. She is very tired of living. Her body continues to defy her and is wearing out. Mary tells me that she thought death would happen suddenly for her, rather than this way, as she becomes more helpless over time.

She has to rely on others for the simplest of things. Some days her eyes don't cooperate, and other days it's her bowels. As she says: "I feel like I'm fighting City Hall."

I watch as her patience with others diminishes, her solitude is taken away by a roommate who blasts the television all day, and her mind fails to the point that she forgets even the simplest things. At times she lashes out with unkind words toward those who are her caregivers, including me.

For the most part, I am grateful to spend time with her, talk to her, read to her, and at times just sit and hold her hand. I see love in her eyes as she looks at me, but her eyes and mind shift as her physical needs take the forefront.

This time of illness is not kind to her. The psychological pain of her loss of independence as well as her physical aches and discomfort remind her of other illnesses and pain in her life.

What Should I Do and Say?

My heart is breaking as I watch my dearest confidante and friend in the final months of her life. What I learn is that this is the time for me to really watch for the things I can do to make her more comfortable and to quietly listen to what she says to me and asks me to do for her.

Listening to another's needs and wants, and acting in a loving manner, takes some practice and patience. In the following chapters, you learn ways to enhance your listening skills.

You bring your own humanness and life experience when you enter the space of someone who is dying. Be patient with yourself as you learn what words and actions can help the dying person.

. . .

The next chapters reinforce the notion
that listening is the most important step
in communicating and being with
someone who is dying. In
PART TWO: Knowing What to Do and Say,
the focus is also on understanding more about
the process of dying and of living with
the person who is dying.

CHAPTER 7:

Actively Dying:
Understanding the Process

In dying, one can plan,
one can be anxious, or one can
just sit quietly waiting for death.
As time runs out, it's in the not-doing
that all becomes clear.

"I thought a person couldn't live more than a few days without food or water."

There is quite a buzz around a roomful of hospice volunteers talking about their experiences with actively dying people. The question to the moderator and expert is about a woman who has not eaten or drunk anything for many weeks.

"We just don't know. Yes, she is still alive but in a coma. And no, she has not been given any fluids or eaten anything for a few weeks."

The next evening I am called to sit with this same woman. As I arrive, Julia is breathing quite noisily, her eyes closed. I am holding her still warm hand as her son enters the room and asks for some quiet time alone with his mother. Later he joins me in a waiting area and begins to talk about her.

"My mother has had a long and quite eventful life. She is a sturdy farm gal who has been in a wheelchair for the past two years and gained quite a bit of weight. I think that she is being stubborn and has enough stamina with her weight and heritage to keep her alive!"

I marvel at this woman who appears to be fighting death. Julia finally takes her last breath this evening.

Questions to Ask Yourself

What is "normal" when someone is near death?

As a person nears death, breathing patterns change. This can be somewhat frightening to onlookers, as the person may stop breathing and then start again. The person's mouth is often open, with breathing through the mouth, not the nose.

It is not uncommon for there to be a rattling-type sound emanating from the person's throat. It can sound like the person wants to cough but can't do so effectively. If the person is in a hospice or hospital setting, I've noticed the personnel often give some medicine to relieve the cough.

Signs of impending death can include mottling, which is a

change of color or discoloration of the skin, on the person's legs. However, with my first hospice patient, although I kept checking her feet and legs, there was never any mottling.

Weight and appetite loss commonly occur, yet I had one patient ask me for a fried-egg sandwich and she ate most of it just a few hours before she died.

You may notice that the person has difficulty swallowing. Usually he or she does not have much interest in drinking or eating, and instead spends most of the time sleeping.

Urine output decreases, and sometimes the abdomen looks swollen. As circulation continues to shut down in the body, the person's feet and hands usually get cold. Yet the hands of one of my hospice patients *were* warm, and when he died, the nurses talked of his body "still being warm."

What might I notice when sitting with the person near death?

The actively dying person may show some of the physical signs mentioned above. You also might notice some changes in the person's levels of consciousness. Dying patients can be in a deep sleep, but might awaken if someone shakes them or talks loudly near them.

As one of my hospice patients was sleeping fairly peacefully, I spoke directly into her ear, since she was elderly and hard of hearing, saying I was there to visit for awhile. She shook herself and asked me if she had to wake up!

Another man I sat with, who was very near death, was surrounded by two daughters and a grandchild. One daughter was quite distraught when it came time for her to go, saying:

"Daddy, I will be back later. Don't leave me." The daughter lingered, brushing his face with her hair and yelling in a panicked tone that she didn't want to leave him. At one point, he opened his eyes, looked directly at me, and winked.

Everyone began to laugh, telling me that daddy just wanted to find out which "pretty lady" was holding his hand. As he lay back down in his deep sleep once again, the family began to laugh and tell stories about him. In his lifetime, he had been quite a ladies' man.

Sometimes you hear about a person "rallying" before he or she dies. A person might hold onto life in order to attend an important event. One friend of mine who wanted to attend her daughter's wedding was able to leave the hospital for the wedding, but had to return before the reception. She died a week later. Another man, who had been in a coma the previous day, was alert during the time I spent with him. We watched television, and then he wanted to get dressed, shaved, and into his wheelchair. He spent the final hours of his life visiting with his friends in the care unit where he had lived for the previous four years. He died within two hours of the time I left him, without any of the signs of actively dying.

I've mentioned just some of the physical signs of an actively dying person. A person can have one, more than one, or even none of these signs.

What are the stages of dying and grief?
In the late twentieth century, Dr. Elizabeth Kubler-Ross first explored the now-famous five stages of grief during the dying

process in her psychological studies after working with dying patients and their families. The stages are: denial and isolation, anger, bargaining, depression, and acceptance.

Denial is the stage in which the dying patient, and even family and friends, declares this diagnosis could not possibly be true. Denial often is the body and mind's mechanism for absorbing the shocking news. It is usually a temporary defense and is often replaced by a partial acceptance. There are a few dying patients who maintain to the very last breath that they "want to live and will live." The majority of patients and families do experience the final stage of acceptance at the very end of the dying process. Along with denial is the dying person's isolating him- or herself from anyone who wants to discuss death and/or dying. The dying person may want to stay in a safe world where the diagnosis is simply not true.

Anger is quite difficult for you to deal with when you are with someone in this stage. Your loved one often lashes out at everyone, and that includes you. One of my dear friends was unhappy in a rehabilitation hospital after breaking her hip. She asked me to read to her while her roommate was watching a loud television show. I continued to read loudly over the noise and at the end of my reading, my friend began telling me that I was a "stupid" reader and talked too much, never saying much of anything of importance. I stayed calm in her presence and later spent time in my car crying. It took a while for me to realize that my friend was not angry at me but at her situation. Anger displaced on you is hard to not take personally. But it is critical for you to understand that *the anger is not about you.* The angry words and actions are about the reaction of the dying person.

Bargaining is a stage used to postpone the inevitable. One hospice worker reported that he never met a person who got out of this world alive! But many of us like to think we will live forever, or don't want to think or talk about death. Perhaps, if we're "especially good," we will get to live for the one last thing we want to see or do.

There are two types of **depression** that you may encounter when dealing with someone who has a terminal illness. The first is focused on being depressed about finances, hospitalizations, treatments, job loss, and circumstances that often occur as a result of the diagnosis. The person may be exhausted, sleep deprived, and in pain. We may try to help our loved one "cheer up" and look at the bright side of things. Words can often comfort someone with this type of depression. Telling a dying person that the house is clean and the children are outside playing happily can be of some benefit for this type of depression, as can having an optimistic attitude on your part.

The second type of depression is not caused by memories of all these past losses but rather, the knowledge of the impending future loss of life itself. Often you may need to be the "holder" of the tears, witnessing the sadness and allowing the person to cry or just sit silently. This is truly a time to adhere to the saying *Don't just do something, stand there* instead of *Don't just stand there, do something.* In this circumstance, you don't need to do anything, simply be there to listen and accept the dying person's sorrow and painful words. Don't think you need to always be "cheery" around the person who is dying.

The last stage of grief is **acceptance.** This does not mean that the person is jumping for joy at the diagnosis, but there is a calmness—the terminally ill person accepts his or her fate and moves on toward dying. On the last day of a dear friend's life, she asked me just to sit next to her and hold her hand. This was an unusual circumstance, since we talked weekly about our friends and all the happenings in our lives. After she told me that she was tired of the struggle, we were quiet for the remainder of my visit. I knew she did not want to deal with my take-charge, cheerful, and often boisterous self.

What to Remember

The stages of grief and dying
(more psychological than physical),
do not follow a step-by-step process—
just as the last hours of life do not always
unfold in a linear progression. Your loved one
may transition from one stage to another at
various times, even within a matter of minutes.

• • •

Pay attention to some of the signs that your
loved one is nearing death. The nurses and doctors
can describe some of the bodily changes for you.
It's important that you make sure the person
is comfortable and relatively pain free.
As a person nears death, pain medication
is often given hourly.

• • •

Some dying people want to be touched:
their hands held, arms or heads caressed, hair smoothed.
A patient's body temperature may change
and you can find yourself fanning the person —
or doing the opposite, covering him or her
with a light blanket.

• • •

Remember to continue respecting the dying person
and talking to him or her as events occur in the room.

• • •

Speak with respect in the presence of the dying person.
It may appear that he or she is near death with
no awareness of the people in the room.
However, hearing is the last sense to leave a person,
so speak kindly and carefully when describing events
and happenings in the presence of the patient.

• • •

Understand that the person will most likely
begin a type of open-mouth breathing
that can sound disturbing to you.
The person's breath may have an odor,
or the body can emit various smells.
Be okay with what is happening.
Often a simple lavender spray
can refresh the atmosphere in the room.
It also has the aromatherapeutic benefit of
relaxing and calming people.

CHAPTER 8:

What Matters Most
in Life and Death

People will forget what you said,
people will forget what you did,
but people will
never forget
how you made them feel.
—Maya Angelou

At the age of eighty-six, Eric is given a two-week "dying" timeline from his doctors. I'm one of the few visitors who comes to sit with Eric, as he is expected to die very soon. However, Eric surpasses his death timeline by four years, past the celebration of his ninetieth birthday.

It all begins when Eric's wife of sixty years dies. He becomes quite ill immediately following her death. Family and friends hold vigils and take turns caring for Eric as his health deteriorates (a heart attack, loss of voice, complications from a fall). Grief over his wife's death seems to have zapped the life from Eric. Death appears to be imminent.

About four years later, Eric and I still visit almost daily. He has become a mentor and dear friend, teaching me about life. He lives each day to the fullest, knowing death could arrive at any moment.

A note comes to my husband in Eric's shaky ninety-year-old handwriting: "Thank you for letting Pris come and check on me in the mornings. She is about the only connection I have with the outside world. Live long and prosper and don't work too hard. Have fun and enjoy life."

I learn about finding joy in the simplicity of life from this elderly man. Learning to cook in your late eighties and waking up for one more day and enjoying the air, the temperature of the day, your home, your animals, and all the people who cross your path is quite an accomplishment.

I am amazed at his patience with his failing body. He faces life with humor and a strong faith. I learn about living in the shadow of death and being always grateful for each moment.

Eric often tells me, "I don't want anyone to be troubled by my death." He maintains his humor and quiet dignity through his last days, routinely chasing a late-morning cocktail down with a dose of laughter. He dies peacefully in his sleep with his two dogs by his side.

Questions to Ask Yourself

What is important to the dying person?

How can someone who is eighty-six years old and in failing health continue to live with that sense of joy and love when others have succumbed to grief, death, and ill health? For Eric, each day brought new adventures. One morning he told me about picking up fruit off the ground with a long, pointed stick. He reminisced about how he used to be able to do handstands and now he could not bend over for fear of falling over!

Sometimes a person may want to be "dressed as usual" and sit in a chair, not lie in a bed. Another elderly, ninety-seven-year-old woman I knew kept a simple daily routine: meals during which she slowly ate, using plates with a light background so she could see and touch her food, as her vision had diminished greatly with age; several naps during the day; using her walker to be semi-independent in the bathroom, where she could wash her hands, brush her teeth, and adjust her clothing with minimal assistance; and time to sit and listen to books on tape. Conversations with friends and reminiscing completed each of her days.

What can I do as the person is getting closer to death?

As the dying person's world becomes smaller, notice that it's the simple things that become important. The person may want time alone to reflect, and he or she may also begin to sleep more. Take your cue from the dying person as conversations become shorter. Ask or notice what is needed: cool water with a straw, lip balm for chapped lips, and as the reflex for swallowing diminishes, use of a mouth sponge or swab to moisten lips. A cool damp washcloth if the person is warm and use of a fan can be helpful. Use a soft voice to read favorite books or sing songs. Play music quietly in the room—some people want to hear the music popular during their youth, or religious or classical music. And silence can be peaceful and restful. For other ideas, read Chapter 18 on Love.

How can someone keep their humor and a sense of well-being and comfort as death nears?

My visits with one elderly gentleman always started with telling jokes. Rather than focusing on his aches and pains, he began our visits with humor. One story we always smiled about addressed the process of waking up in the morning and deciding whether to get out of bed. If you don't feel any aches or pains, then you know you are dead!

My mother-in-law was bedridden for the final months of her life. She would often wake up in the morning very quietly and say, "Well, I guess I am not dead today," as she smiled at my husband, who was her overnight guest each Friday night.

I asked a one-hundred-year-old woman what kind of food she attributed to her long life, and she said, "Oatmeal every day." All of her family was listening and chuckled at her answer. I told her I'd hoped to hear her say, "Chocolate every day."

Each person needs to decide what activities are important to him or her. For one woman, it was time to reminisce about life while I recorded her thoughts in a journal. Life reviews like this are sometimes shared and captured only as private thoughts and, at other times, as a legacy for the people left behind. Always ask the person for permission if you want to use a recording device, and clarify whether or not the information is to be shared with others.

What to Remember

The dying person wants
his or her life to remain
as normal as possible.

• • •

Keep routines simple
and make sure you accommodate
the dying person so that he or she
can remain as independent as possible
for as long as possible.

• • •

Enjoy simple pleasures:
reminisce, watch favorite programs,
listen to music or books on tape
if vision is a problem,
eat food that is tasty,
go outside if possible or bring
nature inside, and sit quietly enjoying
each other's company.

• • •

Ask what the dying person wants
and take cues regarding the length of visits,

and the number and frequency of
visitors and telephone conversations.
The world becomes smaller
as the body prepares for dying.

• • •

Most people agree that
our relationships with
friends and family matter most in life,
particularly during this time.

CHAPTER 9:

Listening with Your Whole Body

Listen.
Be there.
No fixing, no talking necessary.
Cease the chatter of your mind
and with an open heart,
your whole body is present and
aware of whatever is happening
in the moment.

Susan has gone to a care facility daily for many years to feed her handicapped son lunch and dinner. The son, Ron, is severely handicapped after an accident when he was in his twenties. He is now in his fifties and dying.

Early one Sunday, I am called for a hospice visit, expecting to arrive, visit, and support this mother with her son who is near death. When I enter the room, Susan is attempting to feed the childlike man some pudding. As he grunts and shakes his head, he pushes the food away with his tongue, reminding me of a one-year-old baby.

"Ron, you need to eat something, honey," Susan insists. Ron's sister, Carrie, stands nearby and quietly tells me how he was a normal, healthy brother until his accident many years earlier.

As I listen to the story, I begin to feel angry, wondering what I can possibly do in this room where it appears to be "business as usual." Ron does not appear to be near death to me.

I decide to consider what I am feeling, observe the situation, and pay attention to the things that are happening at the moment. I'll notice what role I'm to play and then later take care of my body feelings, which obviously belong to me, not to the situation in the room.

If we find it difficult to try to listen and observe, it may be because we are projecting our personal opinions and ideas about what should be happening at that time. We always bring our background (mine is a former special education teacher, now hospice volunteer), our inclinations, and our judgment of the circumstances (i.e., Susan should not be feeding her son if he is actively dying). When this happens, we hardly can pay attention to the people or the situation.

I take a deep breath and begin to listen with my whole body and think about how I can be of help to this family, without judgment.

Questions to Ask Yourself

What does it mean to listen with your whole body?

This means to put aside your personal opinions and ideas about what you think should or ought to happen.

You bring your own life history and experiences to every situation. Instead of reacting from this viewpoint, take a breath, focus or center yourself, and actively listen to what is being said.

Be an observer of the situation, notice the feelings in your body that belong to you, and act from a place that makes the dying person and circumstance the focus of your attention and actions.

What is my body language saying to others?

Pay attention to body posture and movements, facial expressions, eye contact, and touch. Be authentic.

Check **body posture and movements.** Notice if you are pacing nervously around the room or perhaps sitting on the edge of your chair looking like you are ready to bolt. Are your hands fidgeting? Do you have any nervous gestures that may convey that you are not relaxed?

Note your **facial expressions.** Are you frowning, grimacing, or looking bored? You can examine your face when you take a bathroom break and look in the mirror. Is your smile authentic? You can observe these expressions at a time when you are not with the dying person.

How is your **eye contact?** Can you look at the person? It's okay and normal to tear up at times. If you feel overwhelmed by tears, excuse yourself and return when you feel more in control.

Pay attention to **touch.** Some people like to be touched as death nears, while others simply like the comfort of someone nearby. Ask for permission to hold hands or touch the other person. If the person is unresponsive, use a soft voice to let him or her know what you're doing.

Just as children often blurt out that you are not really paying attention or listening to them, the dying person can sense whether or not you are being authentic in your words and actions. If you are uncomfortable, take a break. I will walk around the building, look in a mirror at my facial expressions, or use some of the focusing rituals that are found in Chapter 13.

Am I really hearing the dying person's words and wants?

My sister's close friend experienced a second bout of cancer. She called my sister, Rosie, to talk about her funeral arrangements. Rosie abruptly changed the topic, stating that she did not want to hear her friend discuss funeral plans or anything to do with dying. Later that day, Rosie realized that she needed to listen to her friend, despite the fact that she felt uncomfortable discussing the topic of death. She called her friend back, apologized, and listened.

Look for ways to handle difficult questions (for example: "Am I going to die?"). Often our inclination is to change the topic to something more comfortable for us. Ask open-ended questions that allow the dying person to talk. Don't use close-ended questions that involve only a yes or no answer. Here are some open-ended questions to use: What do you think? How do you feel about what's happening?

I like to use a probing question that often gives me an idea of what the other person is feeling and thinking about the situation. I take a guess and say: "You seem to be feeling (and add the feeling, such as *angry, upset, sad*) that you are (and add what you think the situation is, like *dying, sick*). Am I right? Am I wrong? Tell me." And then actively listen to the other person.

Pay attention to the dying person's nonverbal communication, such as body language, as well as his or her words. Experts estimate that less than 10 percent of communication takes place verbally. Unless asking for clarification, listen without interruption. Only ask additional questions to help you understand what is being said more completely. You can paraphrase what the person said to make sure that you understand completely what is being conveyed to you. (You can say, "This is what I believe I heard," and then say it in your own words.) If it is something important for me to do in the future, I often ask if I can take notes, and then I read back to the person what I have written.

There is the harsh reality that the dying person will not be around much longer to talk to you or may be unable to talk as death nears. Also, it is not your responsibility to make the other person talk about death. You are always to follow the dying person's lead.

What are some active listening pointers?

Actively listening to the other person is the most important step in communication. Your attitude, eye contact, and total body language need to communicate your complete attention to the other person. Listen without interruption. I admit I often catch myself listening with my "motor running"—which means that I'm not really listening, but instead thinking about the next thing I'm going to say. Try to still your motor.

When the other person appears to be finished talking, often I ask: "Is there anything else I need to know or can do for you?" Pay attention to your tone of voice as you have conversations and ask questions. You are there to listen attentively to the dying person and those involved in his or her care and life. Active listening is a skill that you can practice anytime you interact with others.

What to Remember

Practice actively listening to others in your daily life.

• • •

Notice your body language and tone of voice
when you are talking to another person.

• • •

Pay attention to the words
the other person is saying and also his or her
nonverbal communication.

• • •

Learn to ask difficult open-ended questions
and prepare yourself to really listen.
This is not a time to tell your own stories
but a time to listen to the dying person's
thoughts and wishes.

• • •

Act as if you are calm,
in control and relaxed.

• • •

Hearing is said to be one of the
last senses to leave, so make sure you
always let the person know you are there,
what you are doing, and when you are leaving.
Don't talk about the dying person
as if he or she is not in the room.

CHAPTER 10:

Sitting in Silence

Be in a place of no language,
a place of quiet and silence;
take time to breathe and relax.

Carry with you this place of quiet and silence,
this secret knowledge of serenity.

The hospice volunteer coordinator calls. "Lawrence has no one to be with him when he's dying. No family, no friends. A neighbor brought him to our hospice facility, and now he's near death."

I pack my hospice bag with a music player, some quiet music, lavender oil spray, lotion, and a book to read for my four-hour vigil. Lawrence is a middle-aged man who appears to be sleeping comfortably as I enter his quiet room. A chair is next to his bed; I notice that his mouth is open. There is a raspy sound to his breath and a gurgle in his throat.

He does not give me any response as I introduce myself and tell him that I am going to sit with him for a few hours. Since he is unresponsive, his hands and arms cool to my touch, I decide to just sit quietly and watch him as he sleeps. I have learned to look at a person's facial expression and note if there is any furrowing of his brow. Since there is none, I conclude he is most likely not experiencing any pain as he is breathing. The nurses let me know that he has had a regular dose of pain medicine.

As I sit watching and observing Lawrence's breathing patterns, I notice a subtle change in the sound of his breathing. I watch as he takes a bigger breath and then stops breathing. And just as I think he may have died, he takes another loud breath and begins breathing again in a regular pattern. The stopping and starting of breath occurs a few more times. He finally takes a breath, and stops. I note the time and begin watching for him to begin breathing again. He takes another breath, and stops.

As I sit quietly in the peace of the room, watching Lawrence, a hospice nurse enters to check something in the bathroom. I ask her about Lawrence and she takes his pulse, then tells me that he has died.

I'm in awe of the peacefulness and calmness of Lawrence's last breaths. I feel honored to be in the room with him. I think of him with love and send thoughts of a safe journey. I spend time in the next hours reflecting on life and death, crying for Lawrence and being thankful that he did not have to die alone.

Questions to Ask Yourself

How do you get in touch with the silence within yourself?
Silence is unusual in our fast-paced, often hectic lives. We're used to the constant bombardment of noise. To sit down and pay attention to silence in ourselves can feel unnatural.

To practice and experience the silence in yourself, it's helpful to begin by learning to do a body scan. This allows you to notice what you are feeling inside your body. Often our bodies give us messages that we don't like to hear. Instead, we prefer to keep up our busy lives and are only stopped when our bodies are sick and sometimes cannot even move!

Slow down in your life by sitting quietly without the distractions of television, conversations, or music and notice how various parts of your body feel. Sit up straight, close your eyes, and rest your feet flat on the floor. Notice how your body feels overall and then begin to scan each part from the top of your head to the tips of your toes. Scan your internal organs and note any aches, pains, or tightness. Do not judge what you feel, just take note and go to the next body part.

When you're finished scanning, take a few moments to go back to the body part where you feel the most uncomfortable. Sit quietly and imagine asking that body part what it is feeling, what it is trying to tell you. Allow yourself to have an imaginary conversation with this feeling (achiness, pain, stiffness, and so on). Perhaps you will learn something about yourself. Sometimes the message can be to slow down. If there is no message, notice how your body feels and enjoy the overall sensation of relaxation and silence within yourself.

If you are sitting with someone who is near death, focus on the silence in the room and the silence within yourself. Pay attention to what's happening to the dying person. Notice the person's breath, any movements, and whether your touch is helpful. It's all right to sit in silence and be attentive and present to the other person.

How can I be silent and yet still talk to the dying person?

My belief is that as a person nears death, his or her heart is open and communication is done in silence. It is as if your open hearts can talk and listen to each other. What you are thinking and feeling in your heart is communicated silently and effortlessly.

What to Remember

Practice being silent.
Turn off outside distractions
and be quiet within yourself.

• • •

Learn to do a body scan.
Notice and listen to what your body is telling you.

• • •

Have "open heart" talks with the dying person.

• • •

There are no easy answers
for knowing exactly what to say or do.
You must learn to be okay with that.
. . .
Remember that silence is golden!

CHAPTER 11:

Beginner's Mind

*This very moment, welcome
each event and life happening.
Show up with "new eyes" to see and
an "open heart" to feel and experience
all the miracles of life just as it is...
not thinking too much...
just being.*

*Beginner's mind is the freedom to greet
each moment with wonder and awe.*

I receive a call from hospice to come sit with a woman, around my own age, whose family is afraid to be with her as she dies.

This non-English-speaking woman is dying in her home surrounded by her family. One daughter speaks limited English. I'm expected to arrive at Margarita's home as an expert on dying and to know what to say and do! As I prepare myself for meeting Margarita and her family, I'm reminded of a remark made by a hospice chaplain: "I am not an expert on dying because I've never done it myself."

Many cars and numerous people of all ages are outside the house when I arrive. As I enter Margarita's home, it feels like a big party: dogs barking, people in a living room watching, and talking over, a blasting television, children running inside and out, and food being prepared in a kitchen. My initial reaction is that I don't need to be here. Then I remember to drop my preconceived notions and cultivate a beginner's mind. I focus on being present to what is happening in this home and to be here in a loving and helpful manner.

I enter a bedroom containing several beds, where people are sitting and talking. In one bed there is a small woman covered by a beautiful blanket. She's sleeping, and her pattern of breathing indicates that she is nearing death. I am given the chair of honor next to Margarita.

It's time for me to be "the expert" and sit quietly, holding Margarita's hand and breathing with her. I notice some symbols and statues that tell me the woman shares my religious upbringing. I ask to play some music with songs from that particular faith that I've brought in my hospice bag. The talking ceases, and the focus is on Margarita, as she embraces death with her loved ones surrounding her.

Questions to Ask Yourself

What is beginner's mind?

Beginner's mind is a place in which we focus ourselves and look at each situation with "fresh eyes"—not bringing our past history or preconceived notions of what will happen, should happen, or is not happening. Instead the focus is on the present moment, noticing what is happening at the present time and taking a breath, emptying ourselves of any interfering thoughts.

If you are the end-of-life companion, you need to be there in a loving manner, not judging the situation, but being aware of what you can and cannot do. Beginner's mind can free us from our normal, often knee-jerk reactions or habitual patterns of actions or words.

How can I practice beginner's mind?

For me, being with Margarita and her family was a good time to practice beginner's mind since I did not speak their language. I couldn't explain or talk to family members. I needed to observe and support what they were already doing.

Practice beginner's mind by observing a baby or small child. Follow his or her movements and notice what the baby is trying to do. Don't interfere, just watch, and note when your thoughts or mind wanders. Then bring your attention back to the present moment. This is observing with an empty mind.

Spend time with someone who has dementia. Notice how the person interacts with you and with what's being said and not being said. One time, I was walking with one woman who had Alzheimer's. When she needed to go to the bathroom, she pressed on her stomach and said, "This needs to be emptied." When you are emotionally involved in the situation, it's harder to cultivate beginner's mind. The point is to practice beginner's mind so that it becomes more automatic.

My belief is that the right things will happen if you use your beginner's mind and stay focused on the present moment in difficult or anxiety-producing situations.

How do I keep a beginner's mind when dealing with an angry or upset family member?

In the story at the beginning of this chapter, I did not have to deal with angry or upset family members. Unfortunately, this is often not the case.

To keep a beginner's mind in this circumstance, separate what is happening with the angry or upset family member from the event itself (which is a loved one near death). There are many ways to react to the event of dying, so you need to make sure you are clear that the family member's reaction is not about you.

Beginner's mind allows you to respect the beliefs, values, and personality styles of others even though they may be different than your own. Remember, you cannot allow yourself to get trapped in a family or friend role. Instead, you are the dying person's end-of-life companion.

What can I do when I'm dealing with this upset family member?

Begin by asking questions. The idea is to ask questions from a place in which you are genuinely interested in understanding where the person is coming from (beginner's mind).

Here are some suggestions for questions:

- What's happening with you right now?
- How are you feeling?
- You seem to be feeling (fill in the emotion you think the person might be experiencing such as *upset, sad, angry, frustrated*) because your (*father, mother, friend* or whoever is near the end of life inserted here) is dying. Is this right?

You need to be clear that the reaction or emotion of the other person is not about you. Your voice, stance, and tone must convey that you're paying full attention to that person and are genuinely interested in what he or she has to say. Make sure you keep the other person talking; become a great listener with beginner's mind!

What to Remember

Think with an empty mind, a beginner's mind,
when you are in a difficult situation
with the family and their loved one
who is dying.

• • •

Ask questions of any people who are
upset about the dying person's situation.
Separate their reactions from
what's happening and know that
their reaction is about them,
not about you.

• • •

Keep your thoughts to yourself.
Find a safe place and person to confide in
if you need to share the experience.
Not everyone wants to hear the details of
your time with the dying person,
whether positive or negative.

• • •

The experience of
being with a dying person
is not about you.
It's about him or her.
The dying person is busy dying,
and you are the observer
and companion.

• • •

Trust yourself.
Know that each person you're with
is unique and has something
for you to learn about life and yourself.

PART TWO

CHAPTER 12:

Awareness

Be aware.

Become learners for each other;
words touch hearts, eyes wide open to
new discoveries and possibilities.

Death is knocking at my door. Two close friends are dying, so I feel surrounded by death. Each has a differing viewpoint toward the last days of his or her life. One wants to be left alone and the other is surrounded by family and friends, yet pushes them away.

Ramona is hiding the seriousness of her illness and diagnosis from her adult children. She has been somewhat of a hypochondriac during her life, so her complaints do not appear any different from her usual dealing with any illness.

Jim says he wants to be surrounded by family and friends, but is quite demanding and difficult in his actions and with his words. His family and friends feel frustrated and don't know what to do.

Ramona spends her final days in the hospital, choosing to use whatever pain medication is available and only allowing her elderly mother to be with her.

For Ramona, I keep in touch with her adult children, listening to their stories and supporting their feelings about their mother's final wishes to be alone. We sit in a hospital visiting area, reminiscing about fun times with their mother.

Jim has many family members and friends visiting him. Each family member and friend feels challenged in interacting with him. His health has been declining for an extended period of time. Jim's family also needs support, not only from me but also from professional counselors to learn how to interact with Jim as he is dying.

Questions to Ask Yourself

How can I bring awareness as death approaches?

Since the focus of doctors, nurses, and health professionals is on the person who is dying, it's often distressing and difficult to understand what's going on with family members (and yourself) as they watch their loved one die. Often there's no clear time frame for when death will occur.

Being aware of what's going on is not just about what's

happening for the dying person. It's for you to approach the circumstances surrounding the dying person while being aware of what's happening in the present moment.

Notice and beware of triggers that do not allow you to be there in support of the dying person. The dying person may want to be left alone or push you away, so pay attention to the ways you can support his or her family or friends instead.

What steps can I take to be aware?

Periodically notice how your own body is feeling. Stop and take an inventory of yourself. Then take a timeout. Perhaps a walk can be helpful for restoring awareness. Remove yourself momentarily from the dying person and notice other things, like the weather, or visit a store or park and walk around.

We often do things in such an automatic manner that we don't take the time to really be aware of what's happening inside ourselves and how we are feeling. If you need some time alone, be okay with taking a break and shifting into doing or thinking about something else for a while.

Make a list of things you enjoy doing and do one thing on that list each day. Don't forget to eat healthy food, get adequate rest, and find blocks of time to relax and step away or take a break from the situation.

What do I need to be aware of during this stressful time of being with a dying person?

It's important to be aware of any negative or self-pitying thoughts about the dying person. Find a safe person to share your feelings with so that you can be part of the dying person's final days with support and compassion. Be sure not to overmedicate yourself with alcohol or drugs. Also notice how your words and actions appear to the dying person and to other people sharing the experience. Being with someone who is dying allows you to learn more about yourself and how you act and react.

What to Remember

Be aware of what you can and cannot do
when the person is dying.
Support the dying person's wishes.

• • •

Notice your own thoughts and feelings,
and take timeouts to renew yourself.

• • •

Awareness is not just about the dying person
but is also about how you are acting
and reacting in the situation.

PART THREE:

Taking Care of Yourself

Taking Care of Yourself

*Find your life, find simplicity, laughter, and love—
even in the midst of adversity.*

"Is it time for me to get up yet?" I see my mother peeking into my bedroom in the middle of the night. She has Alzheimer's, a form of dementia, and now lives in my home. I'm her full-time caregiver.

"No, it's not time to get up yet." It's three o'clock in the morning, and my mother is having difficulties determining if it's night or day. Thankfully, she returns to bed and sleeps until her regular 9:00 a.m. wake-up time.

I'm an early-to-bed, early-to-rise daughter and my mother is my opposite. I am learning how to be patient with her as she descends into this crazy disease. She tells me repeatedly, "I think I am losing my mind." And I realize that I need to take care of myself, too. If I don't find ways to regroup and renew myself, then *I* will feel like I am losing my mind.

At 4:30 a.m., my alarm awakens me to begin my alone time at the gym. My husband stays with my sleeping mother while I join some friends for an early morning exercise class. I am relearning those simple things that allow me to continue to be patient with my mother.

According to experts who study aging, living a long and happy life entails a balance among various factors. How you think and feel is definitely connected to how you care for your body each day. Taking care of someone you love who is dying is a challenging task but also one of the great lessons in how to take care of yourself.

Remember to take breaks, eat healthy foods, and take time to nurture yourself in ways that keep up your mental and physical health—all are often challenging when the world appears to "stop" because someone you care for is dying.

Simple activities, like short walks outside to "smell the roses" or any change of scenery, help you see that the outside world continues to move forward. Even though your life feels like it's in a holding pattern while you focus only on the other person, it is important for your sanity.

What Is My Life Like?

Being with someone who is dying can also be an opportunity to ask yourself questions about how you're living your own life and how you think about death. Questions to ponder include thinking about your philosophy of life and death. What is my attitude? How do I feel about life in general?

Look at how you spend your time and money and what results you see as your life progresses. Do you have time for other people, interests, other family members, and your community? What is your legacy?

Taking Care of Yourself

Often if you are taking care of someone else, you neglect to think about yourself. If you don't take care of yourself, you will not be able to take care of anyone else.

• • •

Use the gift of the time left in your own life
to understand yourself and what motivates you.
PART THREE: Taking Care of Yourself
focuses on the person you often forget about
during the process of being with
someone who is dying:
YOU.

PART THREE

CHAPTER 13:

Rituals

Comfort yourself with rituals.
Tap into the simplicity
that resides inside and
outside of yourself.

When I think of rituals, I think of childhood memories of religious celebrations in my family. Yet as I have grown and studied a variety of religions and religious customs, the most powerful rituals I experience are when I witness and am part of someone's death.

In this chapter, I discuss some simple rituals that allow me to take care of myself, both mentally and physically, before or after I have been with a dying person.

For some people, saying a prayer can be a powerful and personal ritual. For others, a mantra or set of words can be comforting. My personal favorite ritual before sitting with someone who is dying is washing my hands and centering myself. By centering myself I mean that I begin to focus myself and my intentions before I enter the room to sit with this person and his or her family.

Sometimes I will spend a few moments after I've washed my hands visualizing that I am surrounded by a circle of energy or light that protects me. I can then widen this circle to include the dying person and any other people I may meet during my time in the room. My intention is that I say the right words and do the right things, and "do no harm" during this special time.

It's important to take care of yourself in simple ways. Get enough sleep, even if this means taking naps. Eat healthy food and snacks, such as quick-energy foods like nuts and fruit. Keep hydrated by drinking water throughout the day. Take short breaks and move around. Go outside if possible.

Longer breaks can also be helpful—such as meeting a close friend for lunch, going to a movie, or listening to some relaxing music. Find ways to renew and rejuvenate yourself. This can also be a time to keep a journal, so that you can write down your feelings about the situation.

As you read about and practice some of the following rituals, please take into consideration your own physical limitations, doing only what feels comfortable for you.

Suggested Rituals

Breathing Correctly

No ritual seems odder to write about than breathing. We all breathe; in fact, this is how we determine whether a person is still alive. So how can a ritual using a breathing technique help us when we're with someone who is dying? When we're in difficult situations and under stress, we usually begin to take short, shallow breaths in our upper chest. In contrast, breathing deeply adds oxygen to the bloodstream and can make us feel awake and alert.

You can pause anytime during the day, even in the presence of others, and take a few deep breaths. This is extremely helpful when you're sitting for long periods of time while the dying person is changing his or her breathing patterns.

Breathing deeply takes some practice. Here are some suggestions: sit in a comfortable position and as tall and well-aligned as possible. You can place one hand on your abdomen to feel if you are breathing deeply.

Inhale through your nose and let your stomach fill and expand outward toward your hand. Exhale through either your nose or mouth, relaxing your belly (your chest should not move at all!). This breath is like filling up a balloon—as you inhale through your nose, your stomach expands. As you exhale through your nose or mouth, your stomach collapses.

It may feel strange to reverse your habitual breathing style, but know that the benefits of normal, full-belly breathing are enormous. You may even feel a little lightheaded, since your body isn't used to having so much oxygen!

After you've mastered this breathing technique, you can begin to practice a deeper breathing technique. This time as you inhale through your nose, continue inhaling until your lungs are also full to the top and your chest is expanded. Then gently exhale. This breath is much like filling a glass of water—as you pour water in from the top, the glass fills from the bottom up. Your breath comes in from the top of your body (the nose), but it fills you up from the lower abdomen first, eventually filling the chest cavity as well.

Learning to Relax

It's important to incorporate effective relaxation activities into your everyday life. Remember that the more you practice relaxation techniques, the better you will become at them.

Here's an example of a muscle-relaxation technique:

- Find a quiet environment. Sit comfortably (uncross your legs) or lie on your back in a comfortable position.
- Close your eyes.
- Begin by physically tensing a part of your body, then relaxing it and letting it go loose. In your mind, say, "I relax my (insert body part)." Often, I repeat this statement, two or three times, ending with, "My (insert body part) is relaxed."
- Feel a wave of relaxation rising up your body as you guide your awareness through each part.
- Each time you inhale, feel a wave of oxygen and relaxation flowing to the body part; and each time you exhale, feel the tension flowing out of your body.

Using Your Imagination

Here's an example for using your imagination. This is sometimes called guided imagery or a visualization exercise.

When you are in a relaxed state (you can use the muscle relaxation technique or just sit quietly for a few minutes with your eyes closed), envision a pleasant scene, such as a favorite vacation place. Imagine that you can see the place, smell the place, and the hear sounds of the place. Make it so real that you feel you're really in that place.

You can begin visualizing a future time when all is well in your life. Or imagine that one or two favorite people visit you in this place and chat with you, giving you advice. Or envision playing or doing some type of enjoyable activity. Another fun technique is doing nothing and letting your mind relax.

Recharging Yourself

Often we forget to move when we're in a stressful situation or feel tense. To feel energized, you can practice standing tall, waking yourself up, or moving yourself even when sitting.

Standing Tall: Stand erect with your feet together, your heels and big toes touching each other. Tighten your knees and pull your kneecaps up, contract your hips, and pull up the muscles at the back of your thighs.

Keep your stomach in, with your chest forward, your spine stretched up and your neck straight. Do not bear the weight of your body either on the heels or the toes, but distribute it evenly on them both. Your arms should be relaxed and by your sides.

Variation: Stretch your arms up. Lock your elbows. Open your palms, keeping your fingers together. Stay in that position for twenty to thirty seconds, and then bring your arms back down. **Waking Yourself Up:** Stand with your feet about one foot apart. Clasp your elbows, inhale, and then stretch your arms over your head. Take your elbows back.

Exhale and take your trunk and elbows down toward the floor, keeping your legs firmly stretched up and vertical.

Pull on the elbows and extend your whole body down. Relax your head and neck. Breathe! Notice if you can touch your toes. Breathe and stretch closer to the floor.

When you're ready to stand up, place your hands on your hips and lead from your chest to stand up.

Variation: If you have a bad back or cannot bend, place your hands on a ledge or a chair at hip level. Stretch forward.

This is a great technique for waking up, since more oxygen gets to your brain!

Moving Yourself When Sitting: Sit sideways on a chair, with your right hip against the back of the chair. Sit on the whole seat. Stretch your trunk up and take your shoulders back. Line up the trunk with your legs. Keep your knees and feet together.

Exhale and turn your upper body toward the back of the chair, synchronizing the movements of your right and left sides. Move your back ribs in. Do not disturb the position of your legs.

Place your hands on the back of the chair. Pull with the left hand to bring your left side toward the back of the chair and push with the right hand to turn the right side away from it. While turning, keep your trunk upright.

Turn your head and look over your right shoulder. Stay for twenty to thirty seconds, breathing evenly.

Exhale and then turn to the front. Repeat from the other side, sitting sideways with your left hip against the back of the chair.

Getting Rid of Tension in Your Neck and Shoulders

Many people hold tension or stress in their neck and shoulders, leading to stiffness, bad posture, and tension headaches. Repeating the next exercises can ease tension, increase flexibility, and tone the muscles. While seated or standing, slowly do each exercise five times. Keep your spine straight, your neck relaxed, and your shoulders facing forward.

First, drop your head back, and then drop it forward. Now, keeping your head erect, turn it all the way to the right, back to the center, then all the way to the left. Next, drop your head forward and roll it around in as wide a circle as possible. Repeat in the opposite direction. Now raise your right shoulder, then drop it down. Repeat with the left. Lastly, raise both shoulders at once, and then drop them down again.

What to Remember

Learn or create your own rituals
to stay healthy.

• • •

Wash your hands
before entering the room
of the dying person.

• • •

Take short breaks to re-energize yourself.

• • •

Practice various techniques
such as relaxation, guided imagery,
recharging exercises, and breathing.

• • •

Be careful when practicing any ritual.
Take baby steps when you're
beginning any new physical exercise.

PART THREE

CHAPTER 14:

Humor

*"Life does not cease to be funny
when people die any more than it
ceases to be serious when people laugh."*
—George Bernard Shaw

"You have never had a pedicure?" I ask my ninety-five-year-old friend, Katherine.

"Not in this lifetime," she responds.

So I decide to learn how to give her a pedicure. I find an electric foot massager that fills with warm water to soak and massage the feet before the pedicure.

Katherine has moved from her independent home to a group home, where she values my weekly visits. I try to think of new experiences for us to enjoy at the group home, since her declining health keeps us from going out for lunch or movies. Katherine has outlived most of her family and friends. Her world now consists of visits from me, her son, and his wife. She also recently added a hospice team of doctors, nurses, health care workers, social worker, and chaplain.

I bring my new foot massager and some lavender oil. I read an article in a magazine on how to give a "proper" pedicure and foot massage. This amateur pedicurist comes ready to give Katherine the best pedicure!

I set up the foot massager, read the instructions carefully, add warm water, and gently place Katherine's feet in the contraption. As I put the plug in and turn the machine on, Katherine starts to move her body and shake her arms. At first I'm alarmed by her reaction. Then she begins laughing and tells me she decided to pretend to be electrocuted. We both enjoy a great laugh. She then tells me numerous stories of her younger days as a prankster!

Questions to Ask Yourself

How can there be humor when someone is dying?

Humor is such a great stress reliever. The dying person usually wants life to continue as normally as possible, including laughter as well as tears. Although we associate sadness and tears with dying and death, laughter is very healing. The atmosphere and feeling changes when you share humorous stories and times. If the dying person enjoys telling jokes or watching humorous movies, you should continue these fun activities.

One of my first patients loved to begin our visits by telling me a joke. I spent time finding funny stories to read to him since my joke-telling skills were not as good as his. I could never remember the punch line of the joke I was trying to tell!

What are some ways to bring humor into the dying person's life?
Make a list of activities that you both might enjoy during your time together. This could include showing home videos, watching television comedies, Internet videos (especially funny pet tricks), retelling fun family or shared stories with humorous endings, buying a joke or short story book, and reading the comics page together.

You can also create your own list.

What to Remember

The dying person wants to feel normal
and laughter is good medicine.

• • •

When we laugh, there is a positive
physiological and psychological
change in our bodies.

• • •

Practice storytelling, telling jokes,
and other fun, light activities
to share with someone who is dying.

CHAPTER 15:

Grieving

You can't prevent the
birds of sadness from flying over your head,
but you can prevent them from
nesting in your hair.
—Chinese Proverb

Grief can come suddenly. The sudden death of my friend Sara's son shatters her life, and she is forever changed. One day Sara is surrounded by the numerous tasks of raising her family as a single parent, but with one phone call, grief becomes an integral part of each breath she takes.

Grief can be a daily part of life. Len grieves daily for many years as he slowly watches his wife fade away. She loses her ability to remember, speak, and—as death approaches—even move from her bed. Both of my friends are mourning great losses in their lives. It can begin with an impending loss like Len's or come suddenly, like Sara's loss of her son. However, the all-encompassing feeling of pain diminishes over time. Someone told me that grief takes as long as it takes. My father died at a relatively young age many years ago, and I continue to think of him often. Now the sadness and grief is more about what he is missing as my children were born and continue to grow up without his physical presence in our lives.

I watch Sara and Len adjust to a different kind of life as they continue to mourn their losses. Grief is part of being human. Remember that if grief does not dissipate somewhat over time, you may need professional help. Part of being human is acknowledging that during difficult times, we can reach out and accept help from others.

Questions to Ask Yourself

What is grief?

The dictionary defines grief as an intense emotional suffering caused by loss, disaster, or misfortune. It's the part of being human that includes acute sorrow and deep sadness. It is the most painful of all human emotions. Feelings of anger, emptiness, guilt, and confusion often occur when experiencing grief. When I sat with my friend whose son unexpectedly died, the world as she and I knew it suddenly vanished.

Grief begins with a loss or impending loss. It can be sporadic—you have good days and bad days. Though my father died years ago, a certain song, a smell, or a memory can overtake me, and I'll find myself sad and crying. Now I can often replace the sadness with a pleasant memory and a smile. When experiencing grief, you may feel mentally and physically exhausted. You may forget to take care of yourself. You may not only feel angry at yourself but also at the person who is dying or has died.

Why must I feel and express my grief?

Not allowing yourself to grieve or mourn your loss can take an unexpected toll on your body. You might begin to have physical symptoms such as headaches, weight fluctuations, or other physical problems. There can also be emotional difficulties such as anxieties or panic attacks.

Grief is a powerful feeling. And just as there are stages that happen when people learn they're dying, there are parallel processes or stages for grieving: denial and isolation, anger, bargaining, depression, and acceptance. This is not an orderly step-by-step process. It takes time to adjust to a new world from which your deceased loved one is missing.

You don't want grief to "haunt" you. Crying or sharing your sorrow with another person or group may be the beginning of your healing.

How can I get on with my life?

At some point, intense grief will end, but there is never an end to the sense of loss. My friend Sara continues to mourn the sudden loss of her son. She is now active in a support group for people who have lost children. She is a compassionate and understanding listener for those parents. She tells me that it helps heal the pain of dealing with her son's loss.

The goal is to give yourself time to mourn your loss and adjust to a different kind of life. For healing to occur, you need time to acquaint yourself with your new identity. At some point, you learn to make the most of your life and the time you have left before you die.

Learn about yourself through your grieving process. It's okay to acknowledge that it may be time for some outside help, whether through a grief support group or working with an individual professional grief counselor.

What to Remember

Grief takes as long as it needs to take.

• • •

Grief is the most painful
of all human emotions.
At some point, grief will end
but the sense of loss never ends.

• • •

There is no standard recipe
or timetable for grief.
Grief is different for everyone.
It is unpredictable and
largely uncontrollable.

• • •

"Normal" will be different
from what you knew in the past.

• • •

It is okay to cry,
since it's helpful to not bottle up your grief
either physically or emotionally.

• • •

Join support groups,
talk to friends,
and get professional help if necessary.

• • •

Time does heal,
but only if you allow yourself
to mourn.

PART THREE

CHAPTER 16:

Letting Go

*Getting over a painful experience
is much like crossing monkey bars.
You have to let go at some point to move forward.*
—Author Unknown

"Would you like to say good-bye to your father?" a nurse asks.
An emergency room doctor has just told my sisters, my mother,
and me that my father has died.

My father was sick for many years. I remember numerous
hospitalizations, surgeries, and emergency phone calls from my
mother regarding my father's failing health. I lived in a constant
state of suspended suspense, never sure if my father would die
during this hospitalization or emergency room visit. Two of my

young sons knew their formerly robust and humorous grand-father as a frail man (still with his humorous approach to life) who often had various machines attached to his body. On the last day of my father's life, he and my mother are babysitting for their two young grandsons. The afternoon is spent playing with the boys; later, I rest with my father before my husband and I go out for the evening. I am pregnant with our third son.

My father's last trip to the hospital emergency room that evening seems almost anticlimactic. He does not want to wake up again in a hospital to find that he's even more debilitated. I don't need to say one last good-bye to my father. I want to remember him alive, not surrounded by machines and lifeless. I already said my good-byes when he was alive.

Questions to Ask Yourself

How do I say good-bye (let go) and not regret my actions?

Saying good-bye and letting go is done in many ways. Sometimes it truly is a verbal good-bye. Saying good-bye and telling the dying person that you love and will miss him or her can be said out loud. Letting him or her know that at some point you will be okay can be comforting to the dying person.

The point is to convey a message that you value the dying person and realize that he or she will not be with you in physical form forever.

Sometimes the good-bye is part of the anticipatory grief. You know the person is dying, but the illness is quite lengthy. You may be able to talk about the past and even make amends if necessary.

Be clear on what you need to do for saying good-bye so that you don't regret any actions or words not said at a later date. For me, I did not wish I'd seen my father "one more time" when he died. That may not be the right action for someone else.

Can I really let go after the person dies?

Memories can be recalled throughout life. Each memory can be an honoring of the person. What happens if you feel you did not have time to say good-bye due to circumstances surrounding the person's death? Some rituals can be helpful. Perhaps you can write a letter to the person saying good-bye, and then burn it.

Other suggestions for letting go, when your grief subsides somewhat, can include doing something symbolic like releasing balloons or making a memory box or video of the person and his or her life. Create your own "happy ending" for saying good-bye and letting go. Use your imagination for the good-bye that allows you to finally let go.

What to Remember

You never leave someone behind;
you take part of him or her with you
and leave a part of yourself behind.

• • •

Let go by creating something symbolic
for saying good-bye to the person who died.

CHAPTER 17:

Forgiveness

Forgive others.
Forgive yourself.
Through forgiveness comes freedom,
inner health, and peace.

"I want to be in the room when my mom dies. I have been the one taking care of her. Now my brother comes when he hears she's dying. I am the one to be with her when she dies."

Laura meets me in the living room entryway and talks to me as we enter her mother's bedroom. She begins to tell me that her brother, who has been estranged from her mother and the family for years, has just shown up and is in the living room of the small apartment.

Laura's mother is being given pain medication by nurses each hour to keep her comfortable as she nears her death. She is sleeping deeply and is unresponsive to Laura and me. Laura's mother now lives in an apartment in an assisted living community. As we sit nearby, she tosses and turns and at times opens her eyes to gaze out the window.

At some point, Laura's brother enters the bedroom and cautiously approaches his mother, who opens her eyes. The scene is powerful: the son tears up, and mother and son gaze at each other. Seeing this, Laura gets upset. She decides to step out of the room and take a short walk.

Almost immediately after Laura leaves, the mother's breathing changes. Her son continues standing beside the bed. The mother's breathing begins to slow, her son steps aside, and the mother gazes out the window as she takes her last breath.

When Laura re-enters the bedroom, she realizes that her mother is not breathing. She becomes quite upset that she was not present for her mother's last breath.

Questions to Ask Yourself

Why forgiveness?

It may be difficult to admit that another person has hurt or disappointed you or that you have caused hurt to that person. We all carry stories within us about the ideal family, the good mother or father, and so on. With forgiveness, the intention is to release the hurt. Forgiveness doesn't condone or accept a serious wrong and doesn't depend on the other person forgiving you.

Forgiveness is focused on taking care of yourself. It is to release from your heart the burden of resentment and anger toward the other person. Sometimes, if forgiveness is part of a conversation, you may be able to talk about the past and forgive the other person aloud, and also forgive yourself for the past hurts and difficulties.

In Laura's situation, she did not get to choose when her mother would take her last breath. Sometimes the dying person is waiting for someone—and perhaps it was Laura's brother—before dying. The brother was a reluctant participant in watching his mother die. One can only suppose that the moment before death was one of forgiveness between mother and son.

Why is forgiveness so important?

Our minds store an incredible amount of memories. We have our own personal history and our feelings toward events regarding the dying person. In this circumstance, I was not there to judge who should or should not be in the mother's room as she was dying.

It was important for me to listen to Laura and her feelings about not being present at the moment of her mother's death. It was important for Laura to forgive herself for not being in the room, and to understand that the mother's decision to die in the presence of her son might have been her fondest desire. Her mother might have been waiting until she and her son could reconcile.

Forgiveness is really about you and how you feel. It doesn't matter whether the other person accepts your apology.

What can I say or do when asking for forgiveness?
Keep your words simple. For example, "I'm sorry if I hurt you. I love you. I forgive you for any past actions or words that hurt me. Please forgive me for any of my past actions or words that hurt you." Be clear and concise. If appropriate, refer to the circumstances. Words asking for or giving forgiveness are often very difficult to say aloud. To forgive and really let go of your anger and hurt is incredibly healing. The interaction between the mother and son in this situation was not about words of forgiveness but about being present and communicating through the eyes and heart.

Sometimes it's not possible to tell the other person that you are sorry for past actions or words. A letter can be written, and not mailed. Create a ritual and burn the letter. It's all right to seek professional help when dealing with your feelings around forgiveness.

What to Remember

Sometimes the dying person
waits until you leave the room to die.
Forgive yourself for thinking
that you can decide where you'll be
at the time of the dying person's death.

• • •

It is not for you to judge
how much time other family members or friends
spend with the dying person.

• • •

"Please forgive me.
I forgive you."
These are very powerful words.
The intention is for your heart to
release resentment and anger
toward the other person.

• • •

Forgiving yourself and the other person
for past actions and words
sometimes requires the help
of a professional.

CHAPTER 18:

Love

We are all weaving a strong tapestry in life:
it is woven of love that connects and supports us forever.

"Grandma, how are you feeling?" asks Emma, the sweet three-year-old granddaughter of my cousin, Joanne, at the Sunday family dinner.

"I feel fine," Joanne replies, looking at all of her grown children and other family members along with some grandchildren gathered around the table.

Emma looks around the table at her mother and father and siblings with a big smile of happiness. Joanne is in the final stages of brain cancer but feeling well enough this Sunday to join the family at the dinner table.

"Everyone, grandma is fine. She's getting better. She feels fine," Emma says. All of us at the table smile along with Joanne and Emma, knowing that fine meant Joanne could sit at the table and enjoy what is perhaps her last family gathering for Sunday dinner.

Questions to Ask Yourself

How can life simply continue when someone you love is dying?

We often want the world to stop and time to stand still. This is a time of remembrance with or without the person who is dying. Savoring simple pleasures, such as a family Sunday dinner, can help us honor a dying friend or relative.

Can you think of other simple pleasures to enjoy with the dying person?

One of the first formal hospice patients I visited was quite lonely, as her eyesight and hearing had diminished considerably. Since she spent most of her time sitting or lying in her bed, I often massaged her hands and feet, a simple pleasure that she was still able to enjoy.

How can I express my love if it's difficult for me to say "I love you" aloud?

I never remember my mother telling me that she loved me. Instead, she expressed her love by making a comfortable home, cooking meals, and sewing clothes.

One Mother's Day, while leaving a restaurant, my elderly mother turned and looked at her four daughters and said, "You know I love you all." We were all astounded to hear the words said aloud. As a result, it became a new ritual for us to end conversations with our mother by saying "I love you." Eventually it became a standard end to my sisters' and my meetings and conversations as well.

Saying "I love you" might not be a habit in some families, but I think most people long to hear these three simple yet powerful words. It's meaningful to the dying person to share loving memories and shared good times. It's part of our human nature to be loved for who we are and for being part of each other's lives.

What if the words "I love you" are never spoken aloud?

There are many ways to express your love. Love can be expressed through your good intentions, your thoughtfulness in doing simple actions, such as making a phone call, sending a card expressing your love, putting together a memory album or scrapbook of shared good times, or a gentle touch. Most important of all is being there in a caring way by spending time with the dying person. However, in some circumstances, stepping away and not being with the dying person might be what you need to do.

What to Remember

Love is shared through memories and experiences.

• • •

Saying "I love you" is powerful.

• • •

Share love through your
thoughts, words, and actions.

• • •

Create a list of loving gestures
that would be appreciated by
the dying person.

Reflections

*Life is not measured by
the number of breaths we take,
but by the moments that
take our breath away.*

—Anonymous

This book has been evolving for many years. It has been painful at times and joyful at other times to recall the many wonderful people who have enriched my life. Each person who allows me to be present to witness his or her death gifts me with trust and love.

Life is an ongoing process, and death is the part of that one process that continues to remain a mystery. The knowledge of your eventual death allows you to be more present in your own life.

My experience of being with a variety of people who are dying has allowed me to think deeply about my own life and death. Reading this book can be a catalyst for you to think about and answer some of the following questions about your own life: How do you feel about death? How do you feel about your own death? What do you think will happen when you die? What steps do you need to take to prepare for your death?

Remember that it's all right, and sometimes necessary, to plan for your own death and to be around people who are dying. Death is a great teacher. It allows you to become more present in your own life, to notice the simple things in life, such as laughter and the love of friends and family. Whether this is near the beginning, middle, or end of your life, you have the ability to look in wonder at your world, the beauty of your surroundings, and the many gifts life brings you each day.

With each death that I witness, I learn more and more to savor the simple moments of my life and to live my own life with courage and confidence.

Glossary

*The following are some commonly used terms
and information that may be of help
when you are dealing with
someone who is dying.*

Types of Living Arrangements

Assisted Living

There are varied types of facilities or homes that offer care for people needing help with daily independent activities. One type of living arrangement consists of apartments or private rooms within buildings where people can live independently, dispense their own medicine, and receive some services. Services can include some meals, light housekeeping, recreation-type activities, and twenty-four-hour emergency services. Often there is a front desk area that is staffed by employees who answer calls and check visitors in and out of the facility.

Another level of care, referred to as a Skilled Nursing Facility (SNF), provides a room for one or two people, with nurses and aides on staff who help the residents with grooming, meals, and recreation. This type of facility is reminiscent of "nursing homes," where elderly people sit in the hallways in wheelchairs. All medication is dispensed by the staff, and residents are unable to live independently.

A group home, often in a neighborhood, accommodates a small number of people (often ten to twelve) who share bedrooms and common areas. It's similar to a nursing home facility except that it's smaller. Depending on the home, a resident could have his or her own private space or share a bedroom with another person. All meals are shared and care is extended as necessary to residents. It is staffed by round-the-clock caregivers, who primarily provide meals, medication, and assistance as needed.

Home Care

In this case, a person lives independently in his or her own home or apartment. Services are provided as needed by agencies or a hospice service. These services can include meals, help with grooming, housekeeping, and nursing (assistance with medication). A hospice team can assist with services at home. In fact, over 90 percent of hospice patients choose to die in their home.

Palliative Care Unit (PCU)

This is usually a homelike facility (*palliative* means comfort) or is part of a hospital unit where people who are dying can come during their final days of life. A terminally ill person may also spend time in a PCU to regulate medication and then return home. Some PCUs provide short respite care for families or caregivers.

Hospice and the Hospice Team

A hospice serves people with life-limiting illnesses, as confirmed by a physician. A shift occurs from hope of physical cure to comfort care so that the person can live life fully, no matter how much time is left. The purpose of hospice and the hospice team is to bring comfort and dignity near the end of life.

Hospice services may vary according to the hospice. Hospices can be for profit or nonprofit. There are more than 5,000 hospices in the United States. Hospices are covered by Medicare and are regulated by governmental rules.

The hospice team members are experts in end-of-life care. The team usually consists of physicians, nurses, home care aides, social workers, bereavement counselors, chaplains, and trained volunteers. A hospice program may include various therapies such as art, music, and massage, as well as medical guidance for resources and support. The team helps to meet the medical, emotional, and spiritual needs of the dying person and his or her family.

Health Care Decisions

Usually a dying person has the right to make decisions regarding the amount and type of health care he or she needs. When the dying person is no longer able to make or communicate those decisions, another person or agent for the dying person is chosen. Documents known as advance directives outline the dying person's wishes.

These advance directives can include Living Wills (usually written when a person has a terminal illness), and health care directives, written at any time in a person's life, such as a Medical Power of Attorney, often referred to as MPOA or POA. These directives are written, signed by the dying person, and witnessed by someone not related to that person. Hopefully, the person makes these choices before becoming seriously ill. A health care directive is not restricted to terminal illnesses and should be written in short, simple statements that reflect the individual's values and choices regarding any life-sustaining treatment.

A Do Not Resuscitate form, referred to as a DNR, can be signed by a person who does not want certain life-saving emergency care to be given outside of a hospital. The form is completed with an attached photo of the person. It is signed by the person and his or her doctor and witnessed. The form is then placed in the person's residence where it can be seen by emergency personnel.

Other Terms

Actively Dying

The dying person has not been eating or drinking for a few days. The actively dying person may be sleeping more deeply with changes in breathing (slower and more irregular), skin color (mottling and blotchiness), and heart rate (slower). Response level to the environment is greatly diminished.

Gatekeeper

Someone who makes sure that "authorized" or approved people can visit or see the patient.

Mottling

This is a blotchy discoloration of the skin surface that is often bluish/purplish. The skin may appear waxen. Usually mottling begins to occur when the body's oxygen supply is being diminished. Near death, it begins at the feet and travels up the legs. Mottling might also be observed on the hands and arms.

Nonresponsive

When a person does not respond to his or her environment, answer questions, or respond to verbal directions, he or she is said to be nonresponsive. The dying person may also appear to be in a coma.

Rattling

This is a raspy or "rattling" type of sound that often accompanies the breathing of the dying person who is near death. As a dying person nears death, congestion can be very loud.

End-of-Life Companion or Hospice Volunteer

Some hospices provide volunteers who sit at the bedside of a person who is actively dying so that the person does not have to die alone.

Other Questions

Who can give medication?

If the person is in an assisted living facility, palliative care unit, or hospital, the nurses or doctors give medication. For a dying person in his or her home, the caregiver is instructed by the nurse or doctor when to dispense medication. A volunteer for a hospice never gives any type of medication. A volunteer's only responsibility is to give the dying person and his or her family support and companionship.

What is a shift change?
If the dying person is in a hospital, assisted living facility, or palliative care unit, the facility is staffed throughout the day and night. Depending on the staff hours, the shift change refers to a change of staff and personnel.

What is the difference between hospice care and palliative care?
Both palliative care and hospice care focus on comfort care, meaning relief of pain and suffering. Hospice care is focused on people who have been diagnosed with a life-limiting illness and have a life expectancy of six months or less.

This is just a baseline that Medicare uses to provide coverage for hospice. The diagnosed person makes a decision to no longer pursue treatment to extend his or her life, and instead enjoy whatever life is left without lifesaving measures. Hospice does not mean that the person is "giving up." Rather, he or she decides to have the best quality of life during his or her final days.

Palliative care refers to relief of pain and other symptoms, including the stress of serious illness. Comfort or palliative care can take place during any type of illness, regardless of the patient's life expectancy. Palliative care can be given at the time of life-prolonging treatment, or can be given during hospice care, during which the person is no longer pursuing curative-type treatment.

What is the difference between a regular medical doctor or specialist and a hospice doctor?

"Regular" doctors or specialists focus on treatments that can provide a cure for illnesses. This type of doctor informs patients and their families about prognosis and treatment options.

The hospice doctor's intention is to make the end of life, when that is near, as physically and emotionally painless as possible. He or she also wants to spare the terminally ill person from futile medical interventions.

Bibliography

*These are some books that I found to be helpful
as I was interacting with families and their loved ones
who were terminally ill or in the final days of life.*

**Living at the End of Life: A Hospice Nurse Addresses the
Most Common Questions**
Karen Whitley Bell (Sterling Ethos, 2011)

The Four Things That Matter Most: A Book about Living
Ira Byock (Atria Books, 2004)

**Final Gifts: Understanding the Special Awareness, Needs,
and Communications of the Dying**
Maggie Callahan and Patricia Kelley (Simon & Schuster, 2012)

Coming Home: A Guide to Dying at Home with Dignity
Deborah Duda (Revised, 4th edition available on her website:
DeborahDuda.com)

**Rituals for Living and Dying: How We Can Turn Loss and the
Fear of Death into an Affirmation of Life**
David Feinstein and Peg Elliott Mayo (HarperCollins, 1990)

Being with Dying: Cultivating Compassion and Fearlessness in the Presence of Death
Joan Halifax (Shambhala, 2008)

Death: The Final Stage of Growth
Elisabeth Kubler-Ross (Touchstone, 1975)

On Death and Dying: What the Dying Have to Teach Doctors, Nurses, Clergy and Their Own Families
Elisabeth Kubler-Ross (Macmillan, 1969)

What Dying People Want: Practical Wisdom for the End of Life
David Kuhl (PublicAffairs, 2002)

Living through Mourning: Finding Comfort and Hope When a Loved One Has Died
Harriet Sarnoff Schiff (Viking Penguin, 1986)

Who Dies? An Investigation of Conscious Living and Dying
Stephen Levine (Doubleday, Anchor Books, 1982)

Author's Note

*The stories in this book are part of my
personal experience being with family members
and people of all ages who were near death.*

Many times I was the only person present when someone died. In some circumstances, I have changed the names of the people involved to honor their privacy. In some cases, family members and/or the person near death asked to be included in this book.

Without these wonderful people allowing me to be part of their final years, months, days, and sometimes only hours, this book would not be possible. Each person and family taught me how to live my life—savoring each moment, friendship, and experience. For this and many more lessons about life, I am eternally grateful.

Acknowledgments

There are so many people to thank
for making this book possible.

I am forever indebted to my first readers—close friends and hospice cohorts who gave me insight into what needed to be said and continued to encourage me to write. You know who you are and each of you holds a special place in my heart.

I am grateful to my family, especially to my husband and four sons, who have grown to understand my commitment to end-of-life work, and respect the time and effort required to develop and write this book. I also have three amazing daughters-in-law and special grandchildren who keep me smiling and laughing every day. From each of you, I continue to learn what's important in life.

I am thankful for my three sisters, who shared in some of these stories and continue to grow older and hopefully wiser along with their big sister. Thanks as well to my Italian family, who provided the inspiration to begin this book during one of my incredible Italy adventures and gave me the time and space to finish this book in my special Italian home.

I appreciate the continuous support of my friends, who added and continue to add the professional touches necessary for developing, producing, and marketing this book. This is the next step in my writing adventure. I could not continue without all of your expertise and love.

A special thanks to those dear friends whose advice and creativity supported me along this writing journey: Maria Muto-Porter, Barbara Feighner, Beth Hennessey Drathman, and Jamie Chavez.

Finally, I thank my mother and father, who saved boxes of my writing throughout the years and encouraged my love of reading and writing.

About the Author

Priscilla Ronan combines her humor, empathy and lighthearted approach to life with an entrepreneurial business background when writing and speaking about issues relating to death and dying. She uses her skills as an end-of-life companion, a life coach, and a trainer to help others be more comfortable when dealing with someone who is dying.

Priscilla's diverse background includes a master's degree in special education with postgraduate work in process-oriented psychology. She pioneered programs for developmentally disabled children, developed a toddler Montessori program, and taught kindergarten, along with being a wife and mother.

She has designed and facilitated adult training focusing on balancing work, health, and family for thousands of employees in various nonprofit and public organizations.

She now enjoys being a full-time writer and speaker on end-of-life issues, finds joy with her husband, four sons, and young grandchildren, and volunteers at a local hospice in Arizona. Her passion is holding vigil with hospice patients in the final hours of life.

• • •

To learn more about Priscilla's work,
please visit www.PriscillaRonan.com.

Made in the
USA
Monee, IL